Schooled

Lessons for
entrepreneurs
who feel
like quitting

Kimberly Pomares

FREILING
PUBLISHING

Published by Freiling Publishing,
a division of Freiling Agency, LLC.

P.O. Box 1264
Warrenton, VA 20188

www.FreilingPublishing.com

PB ISBN: 979-8-9874834-6-6
HB ISBN: 979-8-9881634-3-5
eBook ISBN: 979-8-9874834-8-0

Printed in the United States of America

Contents

Foreword

What an honor to be asked to write the foreword for Kym Pomares's first book, *Schooled: Lessons for Entrepreneurs Who Feel Like Quitting*. Kym is an amazing entrepreneur and today I am proud to not only call her a close friend, but we get to work together on almost a daily basis.

When I first met Kym in 2016 her business was in financial trouble. She had made some poor financial decisions and, when compounded over time, put her on an unsustainable path. She knew changes needed to be made, but did not know what to do. She joined a childcare coaching program and I began coaching her in early 2017.

Kym told me she did not have the money to hire a coach, but knew she could not afford to do without one. She chose to take a risk and dive all-in at trying to save her business and turning it around financially. This choice saved her business, and totally changed the trajectory of Kym's future.

In every twelve-step program the first hurdle they try to get you to do is admit you have a problem, then you must follow actionable steps that are repeated day in and day out until they become a habit.

The first thing we did was develop a game plan for financial success. Kym had to realize that she did not get into financial trouble overnight, and was not going to get out of the hole she was in overnight.

It took a few years, a few tears, and overcoming some fears, but Kym was able to become debt free thanks to her dedication and delayed gratification. Shortly thereafter she was able to sell her business for a nice seven-figure payday.

I have been to Kym's school and saw what an amazing program it was. Her staff loved her and she made a true difference in the lives of so many people in her community.

The best teacher is someone that has learned a hard lesson through personal experience. When I was looking to hire a new professor at our Child Care Genius University coaching program, it was a no-brainer to offer the position to Kym Pomares. Kym now works with our students to help them improve their childcare businesses with everything from finances to exit strategy.

If you are struggling with any area of your childcare business, we recommend you contact kym@childcare-genius.com. You will be glad that you did!

Brian Duprey, the #1 bestselling childcare business book author of all time, having written six childcare business books, most of them with his wife, Carol. Together they own Child Care Genius University, host the Child Care Genius Podcast, and have opened ten childcare centers in central Maine. You can follow them at childcaregenius.com.

Introduction

If you're like most entrepreneurs, you like to read books written by other entrepreneurs. As most, we like to learn how others achieved their success. Entrepreneurs often like to learn from each other because they can gain valuable insights, knowledge, and inspiration from the experiences and successes of their peers. Additionally, learning from others who have faced similar challenges can help entrepreneurs avoid mistakes and make better decisions. Collaboration and networking can also help entrepreneurs build relationships and expand their professional networks. But we find a lot of the answers we're looking for inside the pages of books.

When entrepreneurs write books, they usually share their amazing tales of success. We learn about their unique and incredible ideas, the smart ways they handled money and growth, how they hired and trained the world's best staff, and how they eventually became rich and famous. They bask in their glory. In this way, although these books can be helpful, they can also be discouraging. Why? Because your venture isn't doing as well. In fact, the reason you read so much is that you can't figure out how to make it work. You want to duplicate the success of those who are doing well, but somehow it just isn't happening for you. You wish you were the next Jeff Bezos or Bill Gates, but for the life of you, you're barely hanging on.

This book is different.

While I did ultimately experience success as an entrepreneur, I'm not going to pretend it was easy or pretty. It was, in fact, difficult and ugly. And I'm going to share with you in an honest and transparent way how I was "schooled" in the process. I founded and ran a school for preschool-and elementary-age children, and I did so for thirty years. During this time I was embezzled from, broke and almost bankrupt, pursued by the IRS, and without a clue in just about everything from my finances to marketing to human resources. When I tell people my story, they literally don't even believe it. They especially don't believe that I survived and lived to tell about it. Today, after having profitably sold my company for seven figures, I work with other entrepreneurs who own schools. I help them navigate the rough waters and learn how to successfully operate a school.

Sometimes when I'm consulting with a school owner, their eyes well up with tears. These are tears of sadness because they are working so hard but with little to show for it, but also tears of joy because they (finally) found someone they can relate to, talk to, and find solutions with. They are no longer alone. I hope this book helps you feel the same way. It's important for you to realize that you're not alone, and surely you're not because you found me!

As a business owner, are you experiencing any of these problems?

- Understanding where you are financially.
- Executing a marketing plan that actually finds customers.
- Paying the IRS or a State tax authority.
- Hiring and training staff.
- Relocating your business.
- You can't find funding.
- Dealing with government regulations.
- Meeting payroll and getting control of your cash position.
- Managing staff you don't trust.
- Losing sleep, drinking too much alcohol (Fortunately, I never have been an alcohol drinker).

- Silently suffering from anxiety and depression.

If so, congratulations because you are in good company. I experienced all of the above, and simultaneously. I vividly remember the worst day of my life when my school was relocated into a beautiful new building. It was of course stressful to construct a brand new building from the ground up, and also stressful because my mortgage payment was about to balloon. I needed to boost enrollment, and fast. But I was ready to conquer the world and I was so proud of how far I'd come. Then on the same day the IRS swept in and I was suddenly broke. Broke, and broken.

It was the lowest of lows and it forced me to reassess just about everything at my company and in my personal life. Today, when I look back at what happened, I'm not discouraged or upset. The memories of that day, and the days that followed, are of course bitter. But they are bittersweet because it wasn't until I hit the lowest of lows that I was forced to discover a way out. I was down but not out. Even though I virtually had nothing left, I was absolutely determined not to quit.

What happened next is what this book is all about. I'm going to share with you my mistakes, failures, weaknesses, blunders, and my personal pain. Being an entrepreneur isn't all glory. The stories are from the battlefield, not the beaches. And I'm here to tell you that you can, and you WILL, survive. If I can do it, anybody can do it. It doesn't matter how deep the hole is, there's a will and a way. Together in this book we'll help you find a way.

Sumner Redstone, the innovative entrepreneur and media mogul, once said, "Success is not built on success. It's built on failure. It's built on frustration. Sometimes it's built on catastrophe." Indeed this is a true statement for just about every entrepreneur I know, for at least a part of their experience. So no matter where you are on your journey, I hope you'll learn something from my journey. Let's get "schooled" together and get you out of your hole!

CHAPTER 1

Working on Your Inner-self

We can get a lot of things right, but if we don't get our inner-selves right, we're going to be disappointed with our business.

You won't read many business books with a chapter about how personal trauma and tragedy can affect your job as an entrepreneur. Most business books take a deep dive into everything from finances to marketing to operations, leaving all the personal "stuff" aside. But we entrepreneurs are just like everyone else. We bring our own personal backgrounds and experiences to work with us, and it can impact everything and everyone around us. Until we confront it and deal with it, it may be the biggest obstacle in our path to becoming a successful entrepreneur. We can get a lot of things right, but if we don't get our inner-selves right, we're going to be disappointed with our business.

My life journey wasn't easy. I'll be transparent with you, my childhood was a nightmare. My father died when I was four, I left home when I was young, and my mother was a tyrant. She ridiculed and criticized every move I made. While not physically abusive, the emotional trauma she left tore me apart. I don't recall ever feeling loved, feeling supported, or experiencing joy as a child.

As I grew up and became an adult, I was terrified of failure. In fact, I refused to accept a good job as an audiologist despite being educated for the role. After receiving an offer, I ran away from it. I feared failure and as a result, I skipped from job to job and never allowed myself to be in real relationships with other people. I was smart, driven, and capable. But my inner-self was a mess and it affected every area of my life, not just work.

Childhood abuse can have a wide range of negative effects on a person throughout their life. The specific effects of abuse can vary depending on the type of abuse, the frequency and duration of the abuse, and the age at which the abuse occurred. However, there are some common themes that can emerge in the aftermath of childhood abuse. One major impact of childhood abuse is the psychological harm it can cause. Children who are subjected to abuse may develop mental health problems such as depression, anxiety, and post-traumatic stress disorder (PTSD). These conditions can have a significant impact on a person's ability to function in their daily life. Childhood abuse can also have negative effects on a person's relationships and social interactions. Survivors of abuse may have difficulty trusting others, forming healthy relationships, or feeling comfortable in social situations. They may also struggle with low self-esteem, which can affect their self-worth and overall quality of life.

I learned all of this later, but while in the midst of my struggles I had no idea that my childhood trauma was the wrecking ball of my life. Later when I married, I (finally) began to understand what it meant to be in a real, loving relationship. But even that was a difficult process that was painful for both me and my spouse. I'm grateful that my husband, Paul, was persistent enough to see us through it.

The ironic thing is that my trauma was, in part, the reason I was so driven. In many ways it was the thing that compelled me to become an entrepreneur in the first place. I didn't realize it at the time but my fear of failure is what kept me going. The fear of failure can be a powerful motivator for entrepreneurs as it can drive them to work hard and do their best to ensure the success of their business. This fear can help entrepreneurs to be more focused, disciplined, and determined in their efforts to achieve their goals. It can also help entrepreneurs to be more aware of potential risks and challenges and to take proactive steps to mitigate them. It can help entrepreneurs to be more resilient and persistent in the face of setbacks and challenges. Rather than giving up at the first sign of difficulty, entrepreneurs with a fear of failure may be more inclined to persevere and find creative solutions to problems that arise.

However, this same fear eventually caught up with me. The associated anxiety led to severe depression and a host of related emotional and even physical issues. I was literally suicidal at times, and nobody even knew it. The torment drove me away from practically all relationships at work. Surprisingly, I was still able to keep my business going. So, while my compulsion to succeed helped me as an entrepreneur, I now believe it was a false and dangerous driver. Rather than it being a positive thing, it ended up being very negative.

I finally reached the end of my rope, panic-stricken and unable to cope with life. It was at this point that I reached out for help. I was not going to give up. Somehow I found the strength to admit I was in trouble and needed to get help. It wasn't easy and it certainly took time, but with the help and encouragement of therapy and counseling, I slowly but surely crawled out of my pit. It was during this process that I began to better comprehend who I was and what drove me. I put aside my fears and began to operate out of faith and hope. When I did this, it had a positive impact on me, all the people around me, and my business. My school went from near bankruptcy to a multi-million-dollar enterprise.

I truly believe if I didn't reach out for help, I would not be here today. Clearly my school would not have survived either. When I tell people my story, particularly other entrepreneurs, they often tell me about their own personal trauma and tragedy. So many times they are suffering in silence. With love and care, I always encourage them to open up and find help.

There are several reasons why someone experiencing mental health issues should reach out for help. First and foremost, seeking help can lead to improved mental health and well-being. Mental health professionals, such as therapists, psychologists, and psychiatrists, are trained to help people identify and address the underlying causes of their mental health issues. My underlying cause was my childhood. Yours might be something else. But with the right treatment, it is possible for you to learn coping skills and make positive changes in your life that can lead to a reduction in symptoms and an improvement in overall well-being. Seeking help can also prevent mental health issues from getting worse. Without treatment, mental health problems can escalate and become more difficult to manage. By seeking help now, you can address the issues before they become more severe, which can ultimately save time, money, and emotional distress in the long run. Looking back on my life, I wished that I had been more transparent with myself much earlier. But I'm thankful that I finally did.

For some people, this might be the most helpful chapter in my book. There is much to learn about marketing, spreadsheets, finances, taxes, and human resources, but if you're not healthy, nothing else will be healthy either. And once you get healthy, everything else will become easier. Happy people get more done and are a joy to be around. You'll find that all the other people in your life will become more helpful as well, in terms of helping you achieve your goals as a business owner. Owning a business is hard enough all by itself, so if you're having to work on your business while holding on by a thread personally, it becomes an uphill battle that will eventually cause you to crumble. So get help now and you can experience what I've experienced: freedom from fear, a sense of true fulfillment, and success as an entrepreneur!

CHAPTER 2

You Have No Choice But to Grow

Like everything else in life, stagnation is the enemy of progress, and in some ways entrepreneurs have no choice in the matter.

I realize that not all businesses and entrepreneurs are cut out of the same cloth. Some are more driven than others to grow their businesses and not stay the same size in terms of staffing and revenue. While business growth is certainly not a prerequisite to owning your own business, most entrepreneurs dream of it. I tend to believe that you should always strive to grow your business. You've probably heard this maxim a million times. "When you stop growing you start dying." Indeed there are many embedded challenges when you don't try to grow your business. Like everything else in life, stagnation is the enemy of progress, and in some ways entrepreneurs have no choice in the matter. For example, if you need to add a new staff person, you have to grow your revenue to cover the additional cost.

In this chapter, I'm going to share with you about my company's growth, its sudden and very rapid, yet painful, growth. But I don't want you to get discouraged by my story because in the end I was triumphant. Growing my business was painful, chaotic, and fraught with unpredictable events that tripped me up more than once. But through it all, I achieved growth of more than 300 percent. My dream eventually did come true.

My message to you is that if I did it, you can do it too! It helps to know that you're not alone, and believe me, you're not alone. So I hope this chapter becomes a source of inspiration for you, especially on those days when everything and everyone seems against you. When you're in the middle of it, the battles seem insurmountable. But you will get to the other side!

Again, my business, my school, wasn't always growing. In fact for many years my revenue didn't grow much at all. The stability was comforting but at the same time I always dreamed of owning more. It wasn't until I decided to grow my business that I encountered the most challenges. In reality, I didn't necessarily make the decision to grow my business. I was somewhat forced into it. This is not altogether uncommon as many entrepreneurs are forced into growth by factors they can't necessarily control.

For many years I rented the space from a local church at a rate of only $700 per month. Great deal, right? It was an ideal arrangement and it put me in a comfortable position as a business owner. When you own a school, your space and location is of paramount importance. I had a good space and location, at a good price. But to my surprise, the rug was pulled out from under me when I learned that I was going to suddenly lose my space. I was surprised because I had no warning whatsoever. Although I was somewhat discouraged, I was also forced into doing something I had wanted to do anyway: grow my business. So I began looking for a new space where I could finally build the school of my dreams.

I eventually landed on a terrific location for my school, was able to obtain an SBA loan for the mortgage, and in less than one year I was the proud owner of a beautiful new, and much larger, building that was well suited to house significantly more children. It was incredibly exciting and fulfilling to see my dreams come true. But along with my new success came many new challenges. Namely, my $700 per month rent increased to a $25,000 mortgage payment. That's quite an increase! You can only imagine all the challenges that came along with it. Of course almost all of my other expenses increased as well. I was Noah amidst a flood of new expenses.

Many of the ensuing lessons I learned during this period, which you'll read about in this book, were a result of growing my business. My life, and the life of my business, was no longer stable and comfortable. It was the opposite. There were many days that I wanted to run away and actually regretted my decision. Thomas Edison once said, "I have not failed. I've just found 10,000 ways that won't work." That's so true. But now, looking back, I'm thrilled that I took the leap of faith. There is no better feeling in the world to see how far I have come and to be a part of a fast-growing, successful business.

Some of my biggest challenges are as follows, and I can guarantee you will experience most (maybe all) of these same six overarching challenges.

Financing: One of the biggest challenges for entrepreneurs is obtaining the necessary financing to fund their business growth. This can be especially difficult for small businesses, which may have limited access to traditional forms of financing such as bank loans or venture capital. Entrepreneurs may need to get creative in finding alternative sources of funding, such as crowdfunding, grants, or angel investors. I was fortunate to get an SBA loan, but there are many other places you might also find financing. In my case I put my home up in order to get the SBA loan. I don't necessarily recommend this but it maybe the only way to receive such a loan. Get creative and be determined as it's not always easy and certainly not a fast process.

Hiring and retaining top talent: As a business grows, it may be necessary to bring on additional team members. This can be a challenge, as entrepreneurs must find the right people with the skills and experience to help the business succeed. Additionally, retaining top talent is essential to the continued growth and success of the business, and entrepreneurs must work to create a positive work environment and offer competitive benefits and compensation to keep their team engaged and motivated. My staff quadrupled in size, so I know a few things about staffing.

Managing cash flow: Cash flow is the lifeblood of any business, and managing it effectively is crucial to the success of a growing company. This can be especially challenging for businesses that experience rapid growth, as they may not have systems in place to manage the influx (and often rapid exit) of cash. Entrepreneurs must be proactive in managing their cash flow, including setting up systems to track expenses, invoicing promptly, and negotiating payment terms with customers. I developed a system for cash flow management, using spreadsheets, which allowed me to track all business monies.

Scaling operations: As a business grows, it may be necessary to scale operations to meet the increased demand. This can be a challenge, as it requires careful planning and the implementation of systems and processes to ensure that the business can continue to operate efficiently and effectively. Entrepreneurs must also consider the infrastructure needed to support the business, such as facilities, equipment, and technology. This was probably my biggest challenge and one I had little experience in. However, I learned a lot and leaned on others to help me.

Maintaining customer satisfaction: Customer satisfaction is essential to the success of any business, and maintaining it can be a challenge as the business grows. Entrepreneurs must work to understand the needs and expectations of their customers and ensure that they are meeting or exceeding them. This may require making changes to the product or service offerings, or implementing new systems and processes to improve the customer experience. Any owner of a school will tell you that keeping customers (parents) happy is one of their most frustrating challenges.

Managing risk: As a business grows, it may face new risks and challenges that must be managed effectively. This could include legal risks, financial risks, or reputational risks. Entrepreneurs must be proactive in identifying and mitigating these risks to ensure the continued success of the business.

We've all heard or read the phrase: My overnight success took a long time. Well, my success took me thirty years. Did I sometimes lose patience with it? Yes! Did I sometimes want to give up? Yes! But I didn't give up. I kept moving forward, growing both in my company and in my own personal development. For some entrepreneurs, their big success takes a lot less than thirty years. But I want you to look at me as a testimony that no matter how long it takes, you can grow your business!

CHAPTER 3

Find Ways to Stay Motivated

*All entrepreneurs have a driving purpose.
We're like airplanes. We need wind
to lift us up and keep us going.*

The thing that motivates an entrepreneur to launch out and start their own business isn't the same thing that motivates them to keep going. They are two very different kinds of motivation, and if you can't find a way to stay motivated after you start your business, it's going to be a tough road. Starting a business is hard, but keeping it going is much harder. I know because I've done both.

People often ask me, "Why did you start your own school?"

I think that I started dreaming of starting my own business when I was very young. I was destined not to punch the time clock. For many years though I did punch the clock, and although I wasn't unhappy with my work, there was something deep inside of me calling me to start something I could call my own. If I was going to punch a clock, it was going to be *my* clock. I worked inside of schools for a few years before I started my own school. But when I did, I knew it was time. I was ready for my startup. I knew it would be hard work but I felt prepared.

It's easy to punch the clock and go through the motions, right? You just do the work someone else asks you to do. It can be fulfilling and rewarding, don't get me wrong. But I'm the kind of person who thrives on responsibility and ownership, who really loves the challenges of striving to give my best even without the safety and security of a steady paycheck. Maybe you are too. That's probably why you're reading this book.

Money was not my primary motivator. Independence, flexibility, and control were my motivators. When you work for yourself, you may still put in long hours—in all likelihood even more than you would working for someone else—but you have the freedom to structure those hours how you want. I love the independence and flexibility that only an entrepreneur can have. Control is similar to flexibility in terms of having power over your own goals and productivity. More importantly, you have direct control over your success and livelihood. While calling the shots is freeing, it does of course come with a cost, many of which I will share with you in this book.

But it was about more than just freedom. Also, for me, the idea of legacy was important. As the owner of a school, I could leave a positive legacy in the lives of children. This was important to me because of my own painful childhood. I'm proud that I was able to instill more joy, confidence, and comfort in the lives of children. This motivated me to keep going when it got tough.

As I said earlier, my childhood was terrible. I will spare you all the gory details but suffice it to say, I didn't miss my mother when she passed away. It's sad but it's also the truth. When you don't experience love and protection as a child, you're completely lost, and even into adulthood my mother showed me no love. Why do I tell you this story?

Once as a child I met a friend who had a caring, functional family, and I was shocked when I'd spend time with them. I didn't know a family could be loving. I didn't even know what a family was. It made me sad, but it also gave me hope—hope for a better future. It instilled within me the idea that I could build a life for myself, both personally and professionally. I didn't have to become a victim and just let life happen to me. I could become a person who loves, has compassion, builds positive relationships, and yes, who starts and owns a business. It wasn't easy and I don't pretend it didn't come with more heartache and failures, but I was determined. This was in part what motivated me to keep going.

Each and every entrepreneur brings a different set of life experiences into their business. My life experiences were full of pain. Yours might be the same. Or, maybe you bring a wonderful upbringing and lots of positive experiences into your business. Entrepreneurs come from all different sorts of backgrounds, rich and poor, young and old, some have PhDs while others are high-school dropouts. It doesn't matter either way. But there's one common denominator. All entrepreneurs have a driving purpose. We're like airplanes. We need wind to lift us up and keep us going. What's your wind? What drives you? It's an important question that you need to answer.

When you work for yourself, there is no such thing as 9 to 5. Weekends are no longer "yours." You'll wear many hats and you might go months without paying yourself. I know I did. All the decisions you make, especially the bad ones, are yours to own. Even though you're prepared to work hard, you will get to the point where you had no idea it was going to take so long to get ahead. This is why you need a motivator, a reminder of why you started a business in the first place. Motivation is the workhorse behind your ideas.

Albert Schweitzer once said, "Success is not the key to happiness. Happiness is the key to success. If you love what you are doing, you will be successful." When you're an entrepreneur, you're not always happy. In fact, you are downright unhappy at times. I was suicidal when my business was at its lowest points. But I did love what I was doing. I loved owning a school and I loved being a business owner. And I desperately wanted it to work. So I had to dig deep sometimes and look inward to find what motivated me. I encourage you to do the same thing. Don't forget why you started your business in the first place, and decide what motivates you to keep pressing on!

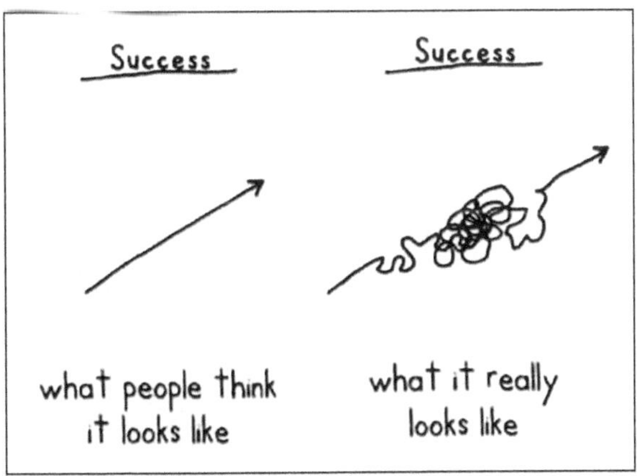

CHAPTER 4

Manage Staff or They Will Manage You

Accept that it will never be perfect, that you will always have problems with individual staff members and with your teams, and that you'll never get as much out of people as you'd like.

Managing people can be a challenging and complex task, and is probably one of the biggest challenges any owner faces. When I started my school, it was just a handful of staff and me. But before long I had dozens and then as many at sixty full-time staff, including teachers, support staff, administrators, and more. I was surprised at the many challenges I was faced with. I always dreamed of having a lot of staff. But it didn't take long before I wasn't quite sure about that dream.

As a manager and as an owner, you are responsible for overseeing the work of a team of individuals, each with their own strengths, weaknesses, and personalities. In order to be successful, you must be able to motivate and inspire your team, resolve conflicts and disagreements, and make difficult decisions that are in the best interest of the team and the organization.

One of the biggest challenges of managing people is dealing with conflicts and disagreements. Even in the best teams, there will be times when people have different opinions or approaches to a problem. As a manager and especially as an owner, you must be able to mediate these conflicts and find a resolution that is fair and beneficial to all parties involved. This can be difficult, as it requires tact, diplomacy, and the ability to see things from multiple perspectives.

Another challenge of managing people is motivating and inspiring your team. In order to achieve success, your team must be engaged and committed to their work. As an entrepreneur, you must be able to provide guidance and support, as well as recognize and reward their achievements. This can be difficult, different people are motivated by different things, and it is up to you to find the right approach that works for each individual on your team. It's never easy.

Finally, managing people sometimes requires making difficult decisions. As a business owner, you are responsible for making decisions that are in the best interest of the team and the organization. This can be difficult, as these decisions can have significant consequences, and not everyone may agree with them. Making difficult decisions requires good judgment, problem-solving skills, and the ability to take responsibility for your actions. It also requires that you sometimes have to terminate staff, which is always difficult and can sometimes have unexpected ramifications, even legal challenges.

I'm sometimes asked what one piece of advice would I give entrepreneurs in reference to managing a team. You might be surprised at my advice. Accept that it will never be perfect, that you will always have problems with individual staff members and with your teams, and that you'll never get as much out of people as you'd like. Frankly, it's rare that you find someone who is 100 percent dedicated to you and your business. If you can even get 80 percent out of someone, you're doing well. This is not a criticism of people. It's just a plain fact. They are not the owners. You are the owner. They won't ever care as much as you do. This is OK and until you accept this, you will continue to be frustrated. I promise once you accept this fact, you will loosen up and not be so anxious about it.

All this being said, you should certainly pay attention to your corporate culture. Building a fun work culture is important for a number of reasons. A fun work culture can help improve morale, increase productivity, and attract and retain talented employees. It can also create a sense of community and collaboration among employees, leading to a more positive and enjoyable work environment.

There are several steps that employers can take to build a fun work culture in their organization.

First, employers should provide opportunities for socializing and building relationships among employees. This can include organizing regular team-building activities, such as group meals, outings, or other events. These activities can help employees get to know each other better and build stronger connections, which can improve communication and collaboration within the team.

Second, employers should encourage a healthy work-life balance. This can include providing flexible work schedules, encouraging employees to take regular breaks, and promoting the importance of self-care. A healthy work-life balance can help reduce stress and burnout, and can make employees feel more valued and appreciated.

Third, employers should foster a positive and inclusive work environment. This can include promoting open communication and feedback, recognizing and rewarding employees for their contributions, and addressing any issues or concerns in a timely and fair manner. A positive and inclusive work environment can help employees feel valued and respected, and can foster a sense of community within the team.

Finally, employers should provide opportunities for growth and development. This can include offering training and development programs, as well as providing opportunities for employees to take on new challenges and responsibilities. Providing opportunities for growth and development can help employees feel engaged and fulfilled in their work, and can encourage them to continue learning and growing in their careers.

By providing opportunities for socializing and building relationships, promoting a healthy work-life balance, fostering a positive and inclusive work environment, and providing opportunities for growth and development, you can create a more enjoyable and productive work environment for your employees. In my experience, this helps to retain team members so you don't have to always be hunting for new staff. It probably won't lessen your daily human resource challenges, but it will make your team happier in their work, which can go a long way toward your own contentment with your staff.

When you start your business you will probably be functioning as your admin team all by yourself. But bear in mind that you want to grow and to grow you will need an admin team that you can depend on.

From the outset, have your eyes open for those individuals that rise above, go the extra mile, and who want to see the business succeed. These people may be who you need to add to your admin team in the future.

Watch them carefully, challenge them to see how they handle additional work and how they function outside their comfort zone. If they look like they will be an asset in the future, pour into them. Support them, give them training, and give them more to do. You want to grow the people that care about your business, who want it to succeed, and are there to support you.

When the time comes that you need to add to your admin team you will have people already in the wings ready to take on the challenge.

A note of caution—you may have good and loyal employees and they may even have been with you a long time. This does not automatically make them qualified to be on your admin team. Don't fall into the trap of promoting someone because they have been with you a long time, they have to be strong, able to learn, and WANT to do the job.

Only promote to your admin team those individuals who "GET IT" (understand what is needed), "GOT IT" (can actually do what is needed), and "WANT IT" (are willing to do what is needed).

Promoting someone because you feel "it is the right thing to do" because they have been with you longer than more-qualified individuals will only create a bigger headache for you to contend with down the road. Promote the people who are going to help you grow your business.

During these post-pandemic days when it is hard to get staff, the tendency is to hang on to bad staff longer than one should. Hopefully, this will be changing before too long. What I want to say is don't hang on to staff that are not giving their best, but right now that is not very realistic. I will say, however, act quickly to get rid of toxic staff before they possibly do irreparable damage. You can manage with staff that is less than devoted to your business but you cannot manage with staff that is actively doing you damage. Get rid of staff that constantly stirs up chaos among the rest of the staff or constantly fill other staff with negativity. You will lose your good staff by keeping them. Further, get rid of staff that is actively derogatory about you to your clients. Keeping them is like shooting yourself in the foot! Clients are going to assume your employees have "the inside story" and are likely to end up going elsewhere.

CHAPTER 5

There IS Help

As a leader, it can be difficult to open up about your struggles and vulnerabilities, but doing so can be incredibly valuable.

Entrepreneurs are often portrayed as driven, ambitious individuals who are able to overcome any obstacle in pursuit of their goals. However, behind the scenes, many entrepreneurs struggle with feelings of loneliness and isolation. I learned this the hard way, and it was quite unexpected. If you're feeling the same way, there IS help. You just have to look for it. But why do entrepreneurs feel so isolated?

One reason for this is the sheer amount of responsibility that entrepreneurs have to bear. As the owner of a business, an entrepreneur is responsible for making countless decisions, from setting strategy and making hiring decisions, to managing finances and dealing with legal issues. This level of responsibility can be overwhelming, and many entrepreneurs find themselves working long hours and dealing with high levels of stress. I felt like I was on the clock 24/7, 365 days a year, and in fact in many ways I was. I think most entrepreneurs find themselves in this same predicament.

Another reason for the loneliness of entrepreneurs is the fact that they are often isolated from their peers and colleagues. Running a business can be a solitary pursuit, and entrepreneurs may find themselves working alone for long periods of time. This isolation can be particularly acute for entrepreneurs who are working on a new or innovative idea, as they may not have the support of a team or established network to lean on. In my case, as the owner of a school, it was particularly frustrating because I was surrounded by not only staff, but by my customers, the children and their families. I had to face them daily, work out many problems, run the school, and all the while feeling like it was me, all alone, who was in charge.

Furthermore, the path to success as an entrepreneur is often fraught with uncertainty and risk. Entrepreneurs must constantly adapt to changing market conditions and consumer preferences, and many face the possibility of failure on a daily basis. This uncertainty can be isolating, as entrepreneurs may feel like they are the only ones who truly understand the challenges they are facing. Despite the many challenges I was facing, I was driven by a desire to create something new and make a positive impact on the world and on children. However, the pursuit of this vision became lonely as I sacrificed my personal connections and support systems in order to focus on my work. I couldn't even bring my work home because it was too frustrating for my spouse to help me with my struggles. Looking back, I don't blame him! But at the time this made me feel even more alone.

When I was at my lowest point and feeling very much alone in the pursuit of my business, I discovered the value of fellowship, comradery, and communication with like-minded entrepreneurs. A piece of marketing showed up in my mailbox extolling the benefits of belonging to a mastermind group and a chance conversation with another business owner led me to investigate joining a mastermind group. At the time I had no idea what a mastermind group even was, but it turned out to be my path toward freedom from the loneliness that pervades entrepreneurship.

A mastermind group is made up of a focused group of individuals who meet regularly to provide support, accountability, and guidance to each other as they pursue their goals. The members of a mastermind group typically have similar interests or goals, and come together to share their knowledge, experiences, and insights in order to help each other achieve success. They may or may not own the same type of businesses. I have belonged to one group of similar business owners and one of very diversified businesses. The important thing is that business owners are all trying to achieve similar goals and have similar challenges.

A mastermind group can be an informal arrangement between friends or colleagues, or a more formal group with a specific set of rules and guidelines. The primary goal of a mastermind group is to provide a supportive and collaborative environment where members can help each other overcome challenges and achieve their goals. When I first joined, I was so surprised that I was not alone in all my struggles and frustrations. It was a sheer joy to discover that so many other entrepreneurs were experiencing the same challenges I was!

One of the key benefits of a mastermind group is the support and accountability it provides. As a leader, it can be easy to get caught up in the day-to-day demands of running a business and lose sight of your long-term goals. My mastermind group helped me stay focused and on track, as members hold each other accountable for making progress and achieving their objectives.

Another benefit of a mastermind group is the collective wisdom and experience of its members. As a leader, it is often difficult to get outside perspective and advice on the challenges you are facing. By joining a mastermind group, you could tap into the collective experience of other leaders and entrepreneurs, and gain valuable insights and guidance on how to overcome obstacles and achieve your goals.

Additionally, a mastermind group provides a safe and supportive environment for you to share your challenges and receive feedback from your peers. As a leader, it can be difficult to open up about your struggles and vulnerabilities, but doing so can be incredibly valuable. By sharing your experiences and challenges with others in a mastermind group, you can gain valuable perspectives and advice on how to overcome them.

Finally, a mastermind group can help you develop and improve your leadership skills. As a member of a group, you will have the opportunity to practice and hone your communication, decision-making, and problem-solving skills in a safe and supportive environment. This can help you become a more confident and effective leader, and better able to handle the challenges and opportunities that come your way.

I remember when I first joined my mastermind group, I was taken aback at how one of the members of our group was not what I expected. He was tatted-up and he threw the "F" word around like it was candy. I didn't expect much help, but I was so wrong. I jokingly referred to him as a "thug." I soon learned he was a genius thug, and an individual I learned so much from. I say this as an important piece of advice: you can learn from anyone. Be careful not to put people in a box and stereotype. This gentleman turned out to be a great source of inspiration and help. He helped save me and my business. Everyone in my mastermind group offered me valuable information on how to improve my business and gave me support when I was struggling.

Joining a mastermind group can be a powerful way for entrepreneurs and leaders to improve their skills and become more effective in their roles. Through the support, accountability, and collective wisdom of the group, you can gain valuable insights and guidance on how to overcome challenges and achieve your goals. There is generally a cost to join a Mastermind group, but the growth you experience can quickly offset the cost.

Today I'm most grateful for the entrepreneurs I'm able to help. I'm amazed at how many people approach me just to say "thanks" for the help I'm able to provide as a leader. It's an incredible feeling that gives me momentum to propel me into the future. I promise if you get involved in a group of like-minded entrepreneurs, you'll stop being so lonely in your pursuits and begin to put yourself in a position to help others who also felt isolated.

CHAPTER 6

There Is MORE Help— Coaching

A good coach can help you recognize the patterns in your behavior that you would otherwise be unaware of.

Beyond getting involved in a Mastermind Group, or in another similar group of like-minded entrepreneurs, every business owner should have a coach. Sure, there are millions of online articles, videos, and other resources on how to build and grow a business. But every business is unique, and a one-size-fits-all solution doesn't always work.

Let me explain. Every business has a different staff, a completely different mix of people and personalities. There's simply no way you can truly go to any outside resource who will understand your staff. Likewise, you are also a unique person. You might be a highly-driven type-A person, or not. You might be a highly-detailed person or a person who is not good with details. You might have good people-skills or you might not like working closely with people. There's simply no way you can truly get the best advice for your business from a blog post or a book because you are original. A good coach can help you recognize the patterns in your behavior that you would otherwise be unaware of. You need a coach!

What do I mean by coach?

A business coach is a professional who provides guidance and support to individuals, entrepreneurs, and business owners to help them improve their business performance, increase their productivity, and achieve their goals. Business coaches use their knowledge and experience to help their clients identify areas for improvement, create actionable plans, and provide ongoing feedback and accountability. They typically work one-on-one with clients or in group settings, offering a variety of services such as strategic planning, leadership development, marketing and sales training, financial management, and team building. They may also help clients navigate specific challenges such as opening a new location, hiring more staff, or releasing a new product or service.

With a good business coach, you'll also gain fresh and new perspectives about your business and the way you run it. It's so easy to get so far into the forest, you can't see the trees. When this happens your thinking gets muddy and you start to make bad decisions. But a coach is standing outside your business looking in. They have a completely different view of things, and as a result they can offer you invaluable insight. In this way, a good coach can help you develop new strategies that take your business to the next level.

So, coaches create an impact by redirecting your perspective on the right path. They change the way you think and act for the better, and this usually provides great results. A good coach:

- Offers an unbiased viewpoint.
- Provides constructive criticism that nobody else can offer.
- Removes your mental roadblocks.
- Recommends new methods or plans you've never considered.
- Assess and evaluate your true financial position.

For some reason, many (even most) business owners don't get a coach. They try so hard to do everything on their own, without any outside perspective. Imagine if an Olympic athlete did that? Do great athletes train by themselves, go to competitive events by themselves, win the gold by themselves? Of course not. Every winning athlete has a coach. Pete Carroll, one of the best football coaches in the NFL once said, "Each person holds so much power within themselves that needs to be let out. Sometimes they just need a little nudge, a little direction, a little support, a little coaching, and the greatest things can happen."

Indeed we all need a nudge. That's what a good coach can provide you with. If you don't have a coach, start looking. It will be the best decisions you've ever made!

CHAPTER 7

When Staff Disappoints

When you trust someone implicitly and then feel totally abandoned and abused, it can take a while to learn to trust again.

Of all the challenges and disappointments I faced as a business owner, none were as difficult as when I discovered that a loyal staff member was actually disloyal and untrustworthy. I'll spare you all the gory details but it involved embezzlement, lying, and of course termination. I was surprised. I never expected one of the people I trusted the most to become my biggest disappointment. Later, as I communicated and befriended other entrepreneurs, I found that I wasn't alone. It's actually not that uncommon for business owners to face this difficult predicament.

One of the most common forms of disloyalty among staff members is the sharing of confidential information. This can include sharing sensitive information about the organization or its clients with outsiders, or using confidential information for personal gain. This type of disloyalty can be particularly damaging to an organization, as it can compromise its reputation and trust among its stakeholders.

Another form of disloyalty among staff members is sabotage. This can include intentionally undermining the work of others, damaging or destroying company property, or engaging in other activities that are harmful to the organization. Sabotage can be difficult to detect and can have serious consequences for the organization and its operations. I would put my disloyal staff member in this category. I had entrusted a lot of information, including financial information, to this person. So the disloyalty was damaging not just in an emotional way, but it literally damaged the organization, which meant my other staff and my customers felt the negative ramifications.

My intention in writing this book is to help other entrepreneurs ward off similar potentially disastrous events. I want to save you from the pain through my own experiences. If you're an entrepreneur and you haven't yet experienced disloyalty, congratulations. But this doesn't mean you should let your guard down, because it can happen to anyone.

So, what actions should you take if you find yourself endangered by disloyal staff?

When dealing with a disloyal staff member, it is important for the organization to take swift and decisive action. This can include conducting an investigation to gather evidence of the disloyal behavior, and taking disciplinary action if the allegations are found to be true. This may involve termination of employment, as well as legal action if the disloyal behavior is severe or illegal.

It is also important for the organization to communicate openly and transparently about the situation. This can include informing stakeholders, such as employees and clients, about the situation and the actions that are being taken to address it. This can help to maintain trust and confidence in the organization, and can help to prevent similar incidents from occurring in the future.

Embezzlement is probably the worst kind of disloyalty. Embezzlement is the act of fraudulently using money or property that has been entrusted to one's care. It is a form of theft that involves taking assets for personal gain, without the knowledge or permission of the owner. It can occur in a variety of settings, including businesses, government organizations, and non-profit organizations, and is often committed by employees who have access to the organization's financial accounts or assets. These employees may use their access to steal from the organization, either by making unauthorized withdrawals or transfers, or by misusing company funds for personal expenses. This is exactly what happened in my business.

Embezzlement can have serious consequences for the organization and its stakeholders. It can result in financial losses, damage to the organization's reputation, and loss of trust among employees and clients. In some cases, embezzlement can even lead to bankruptcy or the collapse of the organization. Fortunately, it didn't get to this point for me and my business, but if I hadn't discovered it, it could have.

To prevent embezzlement, you should implement strong internal controls and oversight. You cannot place 100 percent of your trust in any single individual. This might include regular audits and reviews of financial accounts, as well as measures to prevent employees from having access to financial assets without proper authorization. You should also establish clear policies and procedures for handling financial transactions, and should provide training to employees on how to prevent and detect embezzlement.

Beyond embezzlement, there are a myriad of other ways employees might hurt you, sometimes even unintentionally. For example, sloppy staff might inadvertently give away important passwords. For this reason, it's important you create controls in your business. This is an important part of managing and protecting the organization. Controls are the policies, procedures, and mechanisms that are put in place to ensure that the business is operating effectively and efficiently, and to prevent errors, fraud, and other risks.

There are several key steps involved in creating controls in a business. The first step is to identify the potential risks and vulnerabilities that the business may face. This can include internal risks, such as errors or fraud, as well as external risks, such as competition or changes in market conditions.

Once the risks have been identified, the next step is to develop controls to mitigate those risks. This can involve implementing policies and procedures that define how the business should operate, as well as implementing systems and tools to monitor and manage the risks. For example, a business may implement a system for tracking and reconciling financial transactions, and a process for conducting background checks on new employees.

It is also important to involve all relevant stakeholders in the process of creating controls. This can include employees, managers, and external advisors, such as lawyers or accountants. By involving all stakeholders, the business can ensure that the controls are comprehensive, effective, and relevant to the needs of the organization. Once the controls have been developed, the next step is to implement and monitor them. This involves training employees on the controls, and ensuring that they are followed consistently. It also involves regularly reviewing the controls to ensure they are current and compliant.

Lastly, a word about recovering from disloyalty. This can actually be the hardest part. When you trust someone implicitly and then feel totally abandoned and abused, it can take a while to learn to trust again. My advice is not to let yourself become a victim. If you've experienced it, move forward with confidence that you learned an important lesson, and begin to find ways to prevent it from happening again. If you implement the proper controls, you can prevent this unfortunate problem from occurring again. You'll find yourself being able to trust your staff again, which is important because your staff is your company!

CHAPTER 8

You Can't Please Everyone

No matter how hard you work to make your customers and your staff happy, you will never make them all happy.

When I first opened my school in 1992, I was excited and optimistic. I was on "cloud nine" as they say. I think every entrepreneur feels this way in the early stages of a new venture. I was confident and absolutely sure it would be a smashing success. I had experience in the industry, I was fired-up, and ready to go. I was also blissfully ignorant! What do I mean by that?

My modus operandi was to please my customers, please my staff, please my vendors, and to please everyone else I came into contact with on a daily basis. I thought if I did the "right" thing with good intentions, then everyone around me would be happy. My thinking was that if people were happy, my business would grow. So, I worked overtime to keep everyone happy.

What I didn't know was that no matter how hard you work to make your customers and your staff happy, you will never make them all happy. You can pour love and attention on them every day, but you will not make them all happy. What made matters worse is that I had very thin skin. When you start a business, you often have thin skin. So, I did what most infant entrepreneurs do, I went to even greater lengths to make them happy when they were unhappy. I struggled and felt such anguish when this happened, and it ate away at my sense of confidence.

Let me offer an example. On one occasion early on, I had to discuss the out of control behavior of a two-year-old with his mother. I was very diplomatic and I thought it had gone quite well. She went home and apparently stewed on it. The next day I was informed that this mother was out on the playground telling any mother who would listen that I bought ADHD medication by the jar and was giving it out to all the children. I was devastated! I worked so hard to never lose a client that when I lost clients anyway, I thought I wasn't doing a good job. Each time my confidence took a hit.

It wasn't just with my customers that I over-extended myself trying to make them happy. My staff was very small early on so having good relationships with them was fairly easy. We were like a family. But when the school grew, the staff got harder and harder to manage. When there was unrest or conflict it made me very uneasy and I wasn't always sure what to do about it. I didn't always handle staff situations well because conflict overwhelmed me. Again, my goal was to make them happy, but I can honestly say that it was impossible. I can also honestly say that in many cases they had no good cause to be unhappy. Yet I bore the burden and blamed myself for their unhappiness.

Finally, I experienced the same problems with my landlord. At the time my school was located inside of a church building where I rented classroom space. The pastor of the church and I had a good working relationship. He was pleasant, accommodating, and enjoyed the school being in his church. My clients also became his congregants! But when he was transferred to another location, my new landlord didn't have the same positive feelings about the school or me. We had a poor relationship, and it didn't seem to matter what I did to work on the relationship. It deteriorated regardless of what I did to make it better. This led to my eviction, which came as a complete surprise and I learned about it "through the grapevine." I was devastated! What had I done wrong?

After experiencing more than enough of all this heartache, I finally came to understand that it wasn't my job to please everyone. It wasn't even my job to please all of my customers. Many businesses try to reach a wide variety of customers, but after all, they very quickly find themselves in frustration mode. When I talk with other entrepreneurs, I can see that the logic behind pleasing and satisfying everybody is that if they satisfy more needs or solve a different type of problem, their market will be higher. Because of that, they think there is more probability of higher market share and there will be more probability of success.

The sad reality is that most businesses fail in their first year of operation, and more close their doors after five years. The reason is that too many businesses, mine included, focus on the quick wins rather than setting themselves up for long-term success. They focused on pleasing everyone rather than spending their time reaching their ideal audience, and making the right decisions for the business as a whole and not just a single customer or staff member.

If you spend so much time focusing on trying to please everyone, you're ultimately going to burn yourself out and lose the passion you once had for your business. This may sound like it goes against everything you know and believe, but you don't want to try to please everyone, and you have to be perfectly okay with the idea of not being able to please everyone.

Have you ever heard the phrase "angel customers, devil customers?" Angel customers and devil customers are terms used to describe the types of customers a business may encounter. Angel customers are those who are pleasant to interact with, easy to please, and often return to make additional purchases. They may also refer their friends and family to the business. On the other hand, devil customers are difficult to please, may be rude or demanding, and can be detrimental to the business and its employees. Angel customers are a valuable asset to any business. They provide positive feedback and word-of-mouth advertising, which can help to attract new customers. They also tend to be more understanding and forgiving when mistakes are made, and are more likely to return to the business in the future. Additionally, angel customers can provide valuable feedback to the business that can be used to improve products or services. Devil customers, on the other hand, can be a major source of stress for employees and can negatively impact the business's reputation. They may make unreasonable demands, be rude or disrespectful to employees, or even leave negative reviews online. In extreme cases, they may even try to harm the business or its employees.

Take the time to really think about this. Think about your best customers. Write down a description of them. Write down whether they are male, female, a family, what their income range is, and why they are attracted to your business. The more clearly you can define them, the more you will understand your target market. Far better to focus your marketing efforts on this potential customer than to go after everybody. Wouldn't it be preferable to have a handful of awesome new customers than a boatload of new customers that make your life miserable?

You cannot afford your devil customers, nor can you afford your devil staff members. They take way too much of your time and energy. When you remove as many of these devils as possible, you can then spend time focusing on your business as a whole, and not just a small frustrating part of your business. You'll then be able to provide solutions to your client's problems and be able to show them how to apply them to their everyday lives. You'll begin to create a flourishing long-term business, and finally breathe a sigh of relief! You'll have more confidence and peace of mind.

Stop trying to please everyone!

CHAPTER 9

Embrace Marketing

*When founders and entrepreneurs
ask me how to turn their companies around,
I tell them that highly effective marketing is
a make-or-break necessity for
most small businesses.*

I opened my school thirty years ago. At that time, print advertising, including direct-mail, was the method of choice for most marketing. Periodically, I would place a small advertisement in the magazine section of the newspaper. That was enough to generate interest to fill the small school when it was located in a church. Quietly things were changing in the marketing world but I was so busy running my school, I was unaware of how much things had changed.

When I built my new building and moved, print advertising was no longer enough to gain the attention I needed. When the school was located in the church, I had a capacity of about eighty. The new school had a capacity of 155, and eventually 300. The capacity had nearly doubled, but we were not getting the word out and filling those spots. My meager attempts at marketing were failing miserably.

I probably should not have been surprised that my business was virtually unknown and unrecognized in my community, but it was true. My mentality going into business, when I opened my school, was that everyone would love the school and that the enrollments would come flooding in. Parents needed a place to send their kids, right? I was wrong!

With all the evidence against the notion of "if you build it, they will come," why do founders still believe it works? Why do they still choose this strategy? For me, to begin with, I didn't purposefully choose it as a strategy. I simply chose the path of least resistance, I went with what's familiar. I was focused on managing the school and since I had no real marketing experience, I just let those pieces fall where they may. Then when the pieces fell apart, I was in constant crisis-mode, but still not understanding that part of my problem was that I didn't have a marketing plan. I didn't really even know what a marketing plan was.

For many startups, the work of running the business is so all-consuming that there is little time or energy left to consider marketing. There is also usually little understanding of marketing, so it just goes by the wayside. Building my school took real time, effort, and money. I didn't have much time or money, but I did have a lot of effort. In fact on most days that's all I had was effort. So, I worked and I worked, thinking the harder I worked the better things would get. Rather than discovering what the real problem was, and dealing with the heartache of figuring out the truth, I stayed unaware. No founder would put it in those words, of course. They instead give excuses that their products or services need one or two more features before they're ready to take off. But in reality, the problem is a marketing problem. And that was my problem.

I assumed that people knew about my school. I assumed that people knew it was a great school, that we had good teachers and a good environment. I assumed they knew they could visit anytime to check us out. None of this was true. It wasn't until we were almost bankrupt that I told myself that developing a marketing plan needed to be a priority. Some of this was because other people, wiser and more experienced people, gave me some good advice for developing a marketing plan.

At first I launched into marketing by myself. In addition to running my school, I appointed myself the marketing director. I rolled up my sleeves, jumped on social media, and started posting. I had a shoestring budget but like everything else I did, I wasn't afraid to do it all by myself. This turned out to be a bad decision. I got nowhere and I was increasingly frustrated. I finally turned to a professional marketing agency. My advice to every entrepreneur, if you don't have professional marketing experience, you should consider hiring a professional. Here's why:

First, you need a fresh set of eyes to look into your business. If you're confident in the value your business provides but find it difficult to reach more people that will benefit from it, then it may be time to rethink your marketing strategy. Working with a marketing agency will get you the perspective of experts so that you can create a rock solid foundation for everything related to marketing. That can mean creating a new website, which I did, for a more consistent look and feel across your business or it can mean using new channels to reach a wider audience.

Second, it allows you to spend more time doing what's important—running your business. Outsourcing your marketing efforts frees up your time. Marketing is such an important part of any business, but as a business owner, sometimes it may not be your forte and that's okay. Your goal should be to optimize your time and do what you're best at doing. My problem was that social media was consuming way too much time. But when I hired a marketing agency, it freed up my valuable time so I could focus on running my school.

Third, you'll save money. You probably don't believe me, but it's true. When I received my first proposal from a marketing company, I almost hyperventilated. It was so expensive. But I discovered that hiring a marketing agency will not only save time but also money. Working with a marketing agency is a cost-efficient way to create tangible results within a specific time frame. Yes, you'll be spending money initially but compared to having a dedicated marketing team, you'll be saving more in the long run when you factor in salaries, benefits, healthcare, and even marketing tools. Hiring a marketing agency removes all of these additional costs and will make it easier for you to manage budgets.

Marketing can be expensive. I was terrified of commiting to the expense. But then I developed a method of putting all the numbers in a spreadsheet. The decision then became very easy. This method allowed me to get the "chaos" out of my head, which I will explain in the next chapter.

Finally, you'll get more creative ideas. You simply cannot be creative all by yourself. You need collaboration with creative professionals. When I finally had a team of creative marketing people supporting me, the image of my business began to improve. Suddenly we had a much more professional website and marketing materials. We finally "looked" like a great school, which made me happy because I did run a great school!

A great marketing company serves various clients in one or more areas of marketing, all in an effort to help them achieve their business goals. Most of a marketing agency's functions can be placed into three fundamental categories:

- Identifying marketing opportunities that align with your business goals.
- Executing marketing strategies and tactics.
- Measuring and analyzing the performance of marketing strategies and tactics.

And once they've completed those three stages, they'll take a step back to reevaluate your business goals, then do it all over again—lathering, rinsing, and repeating to strategically drive your business forward. This is how my business finally began to take root in our community. It didn't happen overnight, but it also happened a lot faster than when I was doing it on my own.

Trying to manage your own marketing is extremely challenging. Keeping abreast on the latest social media algorithms alone is a job in and of itself. My marketing agency leveraged ex-Facebook employees to research these, which helped us rise to the top both on social media and on the search engines. I was pleasantly surprised at how much easier my school was to find on the Internet, once the algorithms were properly defined.

I learned valuable lessons before and after I hired a marketing agency. It didn't happen overnight, and, in fact, I fired two agencies before I finally found a good one to work with. Don't be afraid to do the same.

I discovered that I desperately needed marketing, then I discovered I couldn't do it on my own. When founders and entrepreneurs ask me how to turn their companies around, I tell them that highly effective marketing is a make-or-break necessity for most small businesses. It's really impossible for you to be successful without good marketing and sales techniques—that's what brings the dollars in the door. Also, marketing is more than simply letting people know about your products or services. You need to know who your customers are. You need to get so close to them that you can anticipate their needs and desires. Then you need to be able to communicate to them exactly why they need what your business can provide. And, then you have to reach them with that message.

After my marketing was developed and became effective, the enrollments started to roll in. The people in my community knew about us and began to call and visit. Yes, it was expensive, but not as expensive as doing nothing. And in the end, it was profitable. It was one of the best decisions I made to turn my business around.

CHAPTER 10

Get the CHAOS Outside of Your Head

Even the smartest, most intelligent, and hardest working entrepreneur can't plan properly if all the information is inside your head.

In the previous chapter, I mentioned how when I hired a marketing company, I got the "chaos out of my head." I use this phrase a lot when I talk to entrepreneurs. It was a key ingredient in terms of crawling out of the hole I was in and finally understanding my business, and also how to bring it back to life. Let me explain what I mean.

The human mind can solve almost any type of problem, and our creativity can push the boundaries of what's possible. We entrepreneurs are very creative people. But what happens when problem-solving or creativity run wild in our minds? We are so good at identifying problems and imagining scenarios that sometimes it is hard to stop. Do you ever get into imaginary arguments with yourself in an attempt to find answers? Throw in anxiety regarding this decision making and possible outcomes and you have the recipe for a chaotic mind. With a brain in overdrive, it becomes nearly impossible to turn your brain off and allow it to rest.

This is what happened to me. I had stored so much information inside my head that, despite my best efforts and my creativity, I became incredibly lost.

I struggled with repetitive thoughts, overthinking, which led to anxiety and even depression. Sure I had great ideas. But the ideas weren't helping me or my business because I was stymied due to too much information. Much of what makes us entrepreneurs is the way we process outside stimuli and information. We take our surroundings and filter them through our perspective, warping them and shaping them into how they can fit in our business. But too much stimuli is a bad thing.

What did I have stored in my head? Everything from my bills, payroll and human resources, my employees, vendors, and of course my many students. I didn't document much of anything and I thought I was smart enough to store all the details in my brain, sort it all out there, and output it like a computer might. But I got all tripped up and, ultimately, I couldn't make sense of it all. This also prevented me from planning and strategizing because everything was spur of the moment.

This constant state of stress combined with lack of sleep sent me on a downward spiral. I became so depressed that I could barely function. It got so bad that when discussing my business issues with anyone I could barely get two sentences out without breaking down in tears. I could see no solutions to my problems, only an unlimited future of the same depressing daily grind.

I felt I had a tiger by the tail. Everything I owned was tied up in my business. I couldn't foresee the business getting better so I was heading to bankruptcy. But if I decided to let loose of the tiger's tail and close the business I would lose everything I had worked so hard for. I couldn't bear that thought either. Further, I had two college-age daughters that I needed to provide for, how could I let them down?

Living with so much chaos in my head, most nights were sleepless. It's not surprising that during many of those dark and long nights I contemplated suicide. Thankfully, I chose not to act on those thoughts, I couldn't do that to my family.

Even the smartest, most intelligent, and hardest working entrepreneur can't plan properly if all the information is inside your head. And for sure, nobody else can help you if they can't see what's going on. The human brain simply isn't capable of storing so much information. It needs output so you can clear your head and make better decisions. The idea of clearing one's mind isn't exactly a breakthrough. Even

Steve Jobs once asserted that the driving factor behind his creative inspiration was a clear mind. He used meditation.

As entrepreneurs, we're always working, and we grow accustomed to thinking about our business every waking second. But people need a respite from constant mental processing in order to put ground-breaking ideas into action and achieve measurable results. If your mind is so packed with information, you have little space left for creativity. You'll also become a grumpy person and no fun to work with!

Based on the advice from a group of experienced entrepreneurs, I began the process of getting all the information out of my head and onto paper, spread-sheets to be exact. I was a spreadsheet novice and it took me a while, but today I'm an expert and I became religious about using spreadsheets to document and predict everything about my business. Spreadsheets became a cornerstone application for my businesses. If you think spreadsheets are for accounting nerds only, think again. It's the Swiss Army knife of a business, capable of being far more useful than it looks on the surface.

With Microsoft Excel (or any other spreadsheet), a simple column grid approach can help you track all your business's finances and planning. It is fairly straightforward to set up formulas so that the math happens automatically—correcting your totals if you change a figure in the spreadsheet. But that is just the start of what's possible. These formulas can work across other spreadsheets (tabs) and once you start to keep a record of your business, the numbers will tally between pages and your spreadsheets should "speak" to each other. It's like magic! Your spreadsheets will tell you what's going on so you don't need to try and memorize it all and then process it all by yourself.

For example, when I first considered paying for marketing, I was overwhelmed as I saw the monthly fee as beyond my ability to pay month after month. There was just no way I could afford it, I told myself. Then when I plotted it out as an expense I was even more horrified. But when I plotted the expense AND also included what I considered a reasonable number of new students I could expect monthly (once I started using the marketing company) the outcome was entirely different. The decision at this point really did become a no-brainer! To make it more real I plotted a third time in which I included the additional expense to pay for additional staff for the new students. But until I placed all of this information on a spreadsheet, there was no way I could absorb it all. I went from fear and anxiety to purpose and confidence. I went from YIKES! to WOW! You can do the same thing. The decision to hire the company went from an emotional challenge to a clear math calculation.

What information did I begin to track on my spreadsheets? I eventually tracked everything, all of my monthly expenses and then my enrollments, which is my revenue. I documented this data on a weekly and monthly basis and then revisited it on a very regular basis, checking to make sure both the past, the present, and the future were all accounted for in each cell. In this way, I always knew what was happening with my business. It was no longer in my head and I literally didn't have to think about it. This became my lifeline.

Learning spreadsheets is harder for some people than others. If you're not good at math, if you're not a logical or methodical sort of person, you may need help from a professional. But don't let this stop you. Even a good CPA or bookkeeper can help you learn and use Excel or any other spreadsheet. But the point is to document every single revenue and expense item in a very organized manner, and regularly. You should visit and revisit your spreadsheets almost daily. Then, and only then, will you get a true picture of your business. It was probably the most important thing I ever did to turn my business around and get it all out of my head, where it was driving me crazy.

CHAPTER 11

When It's Time to Reap Your Rewards

For many owners, the exit strategy means selling your business and oftentimes retiring. It means (finally) reaping the rewards of your hard work.

An exit strategy is often thought of as the way to end a business—which it can be—but in best practice, it's a plan that moves a business toward long-term goals and allows a smooth transition to a new phase, whether that involves re-imagining business direction or leadership, keeping financially sustainable, or pivoting for challenges. For many owners, the exit strategy means selling your business and oftentimes retiring. It means (finally) reaping the rewards of your hard work.

It had been almost thirty years before I thought seriously about selling my business. That's actually longer, much longer, than many businesses these days. I find that most business owners, even the owners of schools, start to think about selling in much less time. But I enjoyed what I did, especially after I learned the lessons I wrote about in this book. I didn't have a plan to sell it and live another life. But I wasn't getting any younger and, frankly, running a business had become more challenging than it was in the 1990s.

The most frequently asked question I hear from people about the sale of my business is: how did you find a buyer? In my case it was actually quite simple.

My buyer had been a longtime employee. This was of course convenient as I did not have to actively market the business for sale, use a broker, and endure months-long due diligence. Don't automatically dismiss selling your business to someone you already know. It can make for an easier path. But for many business owners, they have to look far and wide to find the right fit. It requires patience and it's probably a good idea to hire professional help, particularly an experienced attorney.

Another frequently asked question I hear pertains to the valuation of the business. How did you decide how much your business is worth? That's also a complicated question and answer. Both a science and an art, valuing a business is notoriously hard. Business valuation is an educated guess at what an entire business would sell for on the open market. Some people use simple valuation formulas like three to five times revenue or profit. But it usually includes an analysis of the company's management, its capital structure, its future earnings prospects, the market value in its particular geographic region, and of course growth potential. Not many buyers want to purchase a business that has no growth potential. In my case, I hired a CPA with experience in business valuation to establish a price range. I did not hire a professional company to value my business. I simply negotiated a price with my buyer, a price that I personally felt comfortable with, and I sought the advice of an attorney. I don't always recommend this path, however, as every situation is different.

You'll find many resources online and in books about selling a business. So, I won't go into great detail about the actual process from a legal or financial standpoint. Instead, I will share with you what most books, blogs, and articles don't share about. The associated mental and emotional issues.

First, the decision to sell a business can be torturous. For most entrepreneurs, it's like selling their baby! They've worked so hard on it, often for many years, and to let go of it can be quite emotional. It's a roller-coaster of emotions to be sure. Some days you love your business and would not think of selling, then on other days you're ready to throw in the towel and move on to new things. It's truly a mixed bag of mental and emotional anguish. My advice is to take quality time to reflectively map out your future, because that's what we're talking about—the future. What are your long-term goals? Do you want to be a business owner three years from now, five years, ten years? What do you want out of life? Also, are you emotionally exhausted from being a business owner?

We all get there at some point. If you feel like your "best days" are over, it might be time to sell. You also want to consider the possibility that you might eventually lose all that you've worked for if you don't sell. There's a balance between being patient and being long-suffering. If you feel like your business may have hit a ceiling, and may have some tougher days ahead, it's time to think about selling.

Finally, a word to those who have experience selling a business and then wonder, "Now what?" Wow, this can be a very challenging time. Again, I owned my business for thirty years. I admit that my identity was wrapped up in my business. I was absorbed in my business for the better part of my adult life. My business was me. Some people wrap up their identity in the business they own, as the success and reputation of the business often becomes synonymous with the individual's personal brand. This can be both positive and negative, as the business can bring prestige and financial stability, but also cause stress and anxiety if the business struggles.

On one hand, owning a successful business can bring a sense of pride and accomplishment, as the individual is seen as the mastermind behind the success. The business becomes a reflection of their hard work and creativity, and can bring personal recognition and public admiration. This was me.

On the other hand, the stress and anxiety associated with running a business can become overwhelming, especially if the business is struggling. The owner may feel personally responsible for the success or failure of the business, and the stress can take a toll on their mental and physical health. Additionally, the business can consume their thoughts and time, leading to a lack of work-life balance and straining personal relationships. This had also been me.

The problem became, after I sold my business, that I lost my identity. I suddenly had a lot of time on my hands, a lot more money in the bank, and no identity. This was a huge struggle for me and a transition. I've spoken to many other business owners who sold their business and told me the same thing. My advice is to be patient with the transition. It simply takes time. Don't rush into anything new. Try to relax, enjoy yourself, and don't make the transition harder than it is. But to be sure, this transition literally puts some people in a very difficult personal position. Make sure to find a good therapist if you feel like you're spiraling out of control in this way. It happens, so don't be surprised.

After some struggle, I finally got to the point where I was at peace with my decision, and I moved on to new things in life, including world travel plus buying a travel trailer and taking more nice trips! Everyone deserves a reward after hard work, so accept your reward and find the new you!